Thinking About Starting a Business?

A Guide on How to Start Your Own Business

By

Gary Thomas

authorHOUSE®

AuthorHouse™
1663 Liberty Drive
Bloomington, IN 47403
www.authorhouse.com
Phone: 1-800-839-8640

Published by AuthorHouse 1/24/2012

ISBN: 978-1-4685-4332-2 (sc)
ISBN: 978-1-4685-4331-5 (e)

Table of Contents

Thinking About Starting a Business?   1

A Guide on How to Start Your Own Business   1

Checklist For Going Into Business   4

     Introduction   4

     Identify Your Reasons   4

     Self Analysis   5

     Personal Skills And Experience   6

     Finding A Niche   6

     Is You Idea Feasible   7

     Market Analysis   8

     Planning Your Start-Up   8

     Protecting Your Business   9

     Finances   10

     After Start-Up   14

     Conclusion   15

Business Plan Outline   18

     The Executive Summary   18

     The Executive Summary Shoud Include: 18

     1.   The Business And Its Industry   19

     2.   The Products Or Services   21

     3.   Market Research And Evaluation   23

     4.   Marketing Plan   34

     5.   Market Research   38

     6.   Pricing   52

     8.   Manufacturing And Operations Plan   63

     9.   Management Team   71

     10. Overhall Schedule   84

     11. Critical Risks And Assumptions   87

     12. Insuranc Need – What You Should Know   89

     13. Legal Structure – Choice Of Business Form   93

     Conslusion   99

     14. Community Benefits   100

II.   THE FINANCIAL PLAN   105

     A.   Loan Description   105

     B.   Capital Equipment List   105

     C.   Pro Forma Balance Sheet   113

     D.   Break-Even Chart   114

     15. Proposed Financing   115

III. SUPPORTING DOCUMENTS   117

Thinking About Starting a Business?
A Guide on How to Start Your Own Business

Developing the business you have been thinking about can be a frightening experience it can also be exciting thing for you to do. If you want to start your own business you will need to develop a business plan before you start your venture.

A business plan can provide the prospective business entrepreneur with a pathway to profit. This outline is designed to help you in drawing up a business plan.

In building a pathway to profit you need to consider the following questions: What business am I in? What service or product will I provide? Where is my market? Who will buy? Who is my competition? What is my sales strategy? What merchandising methods will I use? How much money is needed to operate the firm? How will I get the work done? What management controls are needed? How can they be carried out? Where should I revise my plan? Where can I go for help? And many more.

No one can answer such questions for you. As the prospective entrepreneur you have to answer them and draw up your business plan. The pages of this outline are a combination of text and workspace so you can write in the information you gather are develop your business plan in a logical progression from a commonsense starting point to a common sense ending point.

It takes time, energy and patience to draw up a satisfactory business plan. Use this outline to get your ideas and the supporting facts down on paper. And, above all, let changes in your plan unfold as you see the need for changes.

Bear in mind that everything you leave out of the picture will create an additional cost, or drain on your money, when it crops up later on. If you leave out or ignore enough items, your business is headed for disaster.

Keep in mind, too that your final goal is to put your plan into action. More will be said about this near the end of this outline.

SUGGESTED OUTLINE OF BUSINESS PLAN

COVER SHEET: Name of business, name of principals, address and phone number of business

STATEMENT OF PURPOSE

TABLE OF CONTENTS

I. THE BUSINESS
    a. Description of Business
    b. Market
    c. Competition
    d. Location of Business
    e. Management
    f. Personnel
    g. Application and Expected Effect of Loan (if needed)
    h. Summary

II. FINANCIAL DATA
    a. Sources and Applications of Funding
    b. Capital Equipment List
    c. Balance sheet
    d. Breakeven Analysis
    e. Income Projections (Profit and Lose Statements)
       1. 3-year summary
       2. Detail by month for first and first year
       3. Detail by quarter for second and third years
       4. Notes of explanation
    f. Pro-Foma Cash Flow
       1. Detail by month for first year
       2. Detail by quarter for second and third years
       3. Notes of explanation
    g. Deviation Analysis

III. SUPPORTING DOCUMENTS: Personal resumes, job descriptions, personal financial statements, credit reports, letters of reference, letters of intent, copies of leases, contracts legal documents, and anything else of relevance to the plan.

Every small business owner-manager will have his or her own individual reasons for being in business. For some, satisfaction comes from serving their community. They take pride in serving their neighbors and giving them quality work which they stand behind. For others, their business offers them a chance to contribute to their employees' financial security.

There are as many rewards and reasons for being in business as there are business owners.

WHY ARE YOU IN BUSINESS? _____

_____

_____

_____

_____

WHAT BUSINESS AM I IN? _____

_____

_____

_____

_____

In making your business plan, the first question to consider is: What business am I really in? At the first reading this question may seem silly. "If there is one thing I know," you say to yourself, "it is what business I'm in." But hold on. Some owner-managers go broke and others waste their savings because they are confused about the business they are in.

DECIDE WHAT BUSINESS YOU ARE IN AND START FILLING OUT THE FOLLOWING OUTLINE.

CHECKLIST FOR GOING INTO BUSINESS

INTRODUCTION

Owning a business is the dream of many Americans, starting that business converts your dream into reality. There is however a gap between your dream and reality that can only be filled by careful planning. As a business owner, you will need to plan to avoid pitfalls, achieve your goals and build a profitable business.

The "Checklist for Going into Business" is a guide to help you prepare a comprehensive business plan and determine if your idea is feasible, to identify questions and problems you will face in converting your idea into reality and to prepare you for starting your business.

Operating a successful small business will depend on:

- a practical plan with a solid foundation;
- dedication and wiliness to sacrifice to reach your goal;
- technical skills; and
- basic knowledge of management, finance, record keeping and market analysis.

As a new owner, you will need to master these skills and techniques if your business is to be successful.

A number of the considerations are taken into account, often before the business begins operations, are listed in the next sixteen (a6) pages.

IDENTIFY YOUR REASONS

As a first and often overlooked step, ask yourself why you want to own your own business. Check each of the reasons that apply to you.

		YES
1.	Freedom from the 9-5 daily work routine.	_____
2.	Being your own boss.	_____
3.	Doing what you want when you want to do it.	_____
4.	Improving your standard of living.	_____
5.	You are bored with your present job.	_____
6.	You have a product or service for which you Feel there is demand.	_____

Some reasons are better than others, non are wrong; however, be aware that there are tradeoffs. For example, you can escape the 9-5 daily routine, but you may replace it with a 6 AM to 10 PM routine.

SELF ANALYSIS

Going into business requires certain personal characteristics. This portion of the checklist deals with you, the individual. These questions require serious thought. Try to be objective. Remember, it is your future that is at stake!

Personal Characteristics

	YES	NO
1. Are you a leader?	___	___
2. Do you like to make your own decisions?	___	___
3. Do others turn to you for help in making decisions?	___	___
4. Do you enjoy competition?	___	___
5. Do you have will power and self discipline?	___	___
6. Do you plan ahead?	___	___
7. Do you like people?	___	___
8. Do you get along well with others?	___	___

Personal Conditions

This next group of questions, though brief, is vitally important to the success of your plan. It covers the physical, emotional and financial strains you will encounter in starting a new business.

	YES	NO
1. Are you aware that running your own business may? Require working 12-15 hours a day, six days a week, and maybe even Sundays and holidays?	___	___
2. Do you have the physical stamina to handle the workload and schedule?	___	___
3. Do you have the emotional strength to withstand the strain?	___	___
4. Are you prepared, if needed, to temporarily lower Your standard of living until your business is firmly established?	___	___
5. Is your family prepared to go along with the strains? They, too must bear?	___	___
6. Are you prepared to lose your savings?	___	___

PERSONAL SKILLS AND EXPERIENCE

Certain skills and experience are critical to the success of a business. Since it is unlikely that you possess all of the skills and experience needed, you'll need to hire personnel to supply those you lack. There are some basic and special skills you will need for your particular business.

By answering the following questions, you can identify the skills you possess and those you lack (your strengths and weakness).

	YES	NO
1. Do you know what basic skills you will need? In order to have a successful business?	_____	_____
2. Do you possess those skills?	_____	_____
3. When hiring personnel, will you be able to determine if the applicants' skills meet the requirements for the positions you are filling?	_____	_____
4. Have you worked in a managerial or supervisory? capacity?	_____	_____
5. Have you ever worked in a business similar? To the one you want to start?	_____	_____
6. Have you had any business training in school?	_____	_____
7. If you discover you don't have the basic skills needed for your business, will you be willing to delay your plans until you've acquired the necessary skills?	_____	_____

FINDING A NICHE

Small businesses range in size from a manufacturer with many employees and millions of dollars in equipment to the lone mechanic with tools. Obviously, the knowledge and skills required for these two extremes are far apart, but they have one thing in common—each has found a business niche and is successfully filling it.

The most crucial problems you will face in your early planning will be to find your niche and determine the feasibility of your idea. "Get into the right business at the right time" is very good advice however, following that advice may be difficult. Many entrepreneurs plunge into a business venture so blinded by the dream that they fail to thoroughly evaluate its potential.

Before you invest time, effort and money, the following exercise will help you separate sound ideas from those bearing a high potential for failure.

IS YOU IDEA FEASIBLE

1. Identify and briefly describe the business you plan to start.

_____

_____

_____

_____

_____

_____

_____

2. Identify the product or service you plan to sell.

_____

_____

_____

_____

_____

_____

_____

		YES	NO
3.	Does your product or services satisfy and unfilled need?	_____	_____
4.	Will your product or service, service an existing market in which demand exceeds supply?	_____	_____
5.	Will your product or service be competitive based on its quality, selection, price or location?	_____	_____

Answering yes to any of these questions means you are on the right track; a negative answer means the road ahead could be rough.

MARKET ANALYSIS

For a small business to be successful, the owner must know the market. To learn the market, you must analyze it, a process that takes time and effort. You don't have to be a trained statistician to analyze the marketplace nor does the analysis have to be costly.

Analyzing the market is a way to gather facts about potential customers and to determine the demand for your product or service. The more information you gather, the greater your chance of capturing a segment of the market. Know the market before investing you time and money in any business venture.

These questions will help you collect the information necessary to analyze your market and determine if your product or service will sell.

	YES	NO
1. Do you know who your customers will be ?	_____	_____
2. Do you understand their needs and desires?	_____	_____
3. Do you know where they live?	_____	_____
4. Will you be offering the kind of products or services that they will buy?	_____	_____
5. Will your prices be competitive in quality and value?	_____	_____
6. Will you promotional program be effective?	_____	_____
7. Do you understand how your business compares with your competitors?	_____	_____
8. Will your business e conveniently located for the people you plan to serve?	_____	_____

This brief exercise will give you a good idea of the kind of market planning you need to do. An answer of "no" indicates a weakness in your plan, so do your research until you can answer each question with a "yes."

PLANNING YOUR START-UP

So far, this checklist has helped you identify questions and problems you will face in converting your ideas into reality, and in determining if your idea is feasible. Through self analysis you have learned of your personal qualifications and deficiencies, and through market analysis you have learned if there is a demand for your product or services.

The following questions are grouped according to function.
They are designed to help you prepare for "Opening Day."

Name and Legal Structure

	YES	NO
1. Have you chosen a name for your business?	_____	_____
2. Have you chosen to operate as a sole proprietorship, Partnership or corporation?	_____	_____

Your business and the Law

A person in business is not expected to be a lawyer, but each business owner should have a basic knowledge of laws affecting the business. Here are some of the legal matters you should be acquainted with:

	YES	NO
1. Do you know which licenses and permits you may need to operate your business?	___	___
2. Do you know the business laws you will have to obey?	___	___
3. Do you know a lawyer who can advise you and help you with legal papers?	___	___
4. Are you aware of:	___	___
– Occupational Safety and Health requirements (OSHA)	___	___
– Regulations covering hazardous materials?	___	___
– Local ordinances covering signs, snow removal, etc.?	___	___
– Federal Tax Code provisions pertaining to small business?	___	___
– Federal regulations on withholding taxes and Social Security?	___	___
– State Workers' compensation laws?	___	___

PROTECTING YOUR BUSINESS

It is becoming increasingly important that attention be given to security and insurance protection for your business.

There are several areas that should be covered. Have you examined the following categories of risk protection?

	YES	NO
– Fire	___	___
– Theft	___	___
– Robbery	___	___
– Vandalism	___	___
– Accident liability	___	___

Discuss the types of coverage you will need and make a careful comparison of rates and coverage with several insurance agents before making a final decision.

Business Premises and Locations

	YES	NO
1. Have you found a suitable building in a location convenient for your customers?	___	___

2. Have you made a Merchandise Plan based upon estimated sales, to determine the amount of inventory you will need to control purchases?   _____   _____
3. Have you considered renting or leasing with an option to buy?   _____   _____
4. Will you have a lawyer check the zoning regulations and lease?   _____   _____

Merchandise

	YES	NO

1. Have you decided which items you will sell or produce, or what service(s) you will provide?   _____   _____
2. Have you made a Merchandise Plan based upon estimated sales, to determine the amount of inventory you will need to control purchases?   _____   _____
3. Have you found reliable suppliers who will assist in the start up?   _____   _____
4. Have you compared the prices, quality and credit terms of of suppliers?   _____   _____

<u>Business Records</u>

	YES	NO

1. Are you prepared to maintain complete records of sales, income and expenses, accounts payable and receivable?   _____   _____
2. Have you determined how to handle payroll records, tax reports and payments?   _____   _____
3. Do you now what financial reports should be prepared and how to prepare them?   _____   _____

<u>FINANCES</u>

A large number of small businesses fail each year. There are a number of reasons for these failures, but one of the main reasons is insufficient funds. Too many entrepreneurs try to start and operate a business without sufficient capital (money). To avoid this dilemma, you can review your situation by answering these three questions.

1. How much money do you have?
2. How much money will you need to start your business?
3. How much money will you need to stay in business?

Use the following charts to answer the first questions?

CHART 1
PERSONAL FINANCIAL STATEMENT

_____ , 19 _____

ASSETS   LIABILITIES

Cash on hand   _____   Accounts Payable   _____
Savings Account   _____   Notes payable   _____
Stocks, bonds   Notes payable   _____
Securities   _____   Contracts payable   _____
Accounts/Notes
Receivable   _____   Taxes   _____
Real Estate   _____   Real Estate Loans   _____
Life Insurance   Other liabilities   _____
(cash value)   _____   Automobile/
other liquid assets   _____   other vehicles   _____

Total Assets   _____   Total Liabilities   _____

NET WORTH (ASSETS MINUS LIABILITIES)

This next chart will help answer the second question—how much money will you need to start your business? The chart is for a retail business—items will vary for service, construction and manufacturing firms.

CHART 2
START-UP COST ESTIMATES

Decorating, Remodeling   _____
Fixtures, Equipment   _____
Installing Fixtures, Equipment   _____
Services, Supplies   _____
Beginning Inventory Cost   _____
Legal, Professional Fees   _____
Licenses, Permits   _____
Telephone Utility Deposit   _____
Insurance   _____
Signs   _____
Advertising For Opening   _____
Unanticipated Expenses   _____

TOTAL   START-UP COSTS   _____

The answer to the third question (How much money will you need to stay in business?) must be divided into two parts-immediate costs and future costs.

From the moment the door to your new business opens, a certain amount of income will undoubtedly come in. However, this income should not be projected in your operating expenses. You will need enough money available to cover costs for at least the first three months of operation. Chart 3 will help you project your operating expenses on a monthly basis.

CHART 3
EXPENSES FOR ONE MONTH

Your living cost   _____

Employee Wages   _____

Rent   _____

Advertising   _____

Supplies   _____

Utilities   _____

Insurance   _____

Taxes   _____

Maintenance   _____

Delivery/Transportation   _____

Miscellaneous   _____

TOTAL   _____

Now multiply the total of Chart 3 by three. This is the amount of cash you will need to cover operating expenses for three months. Deposit this amount in a savings account before opening your business. Use it only for those purposes listed in the above chart because this money will ensure that you will be able to continue in business during the crucial early stages.

By adding the total start-up cost (Chart 2) to the total expenses for three months (three times total cost on Chart 3,) you can learn what the estimated costs will be to start and operate your business for three months. By subtracting the totals of Chart 2 and 3 from the amount of available (Chart 1), you can determine the amount of additional financing you may need, if any.

How, you will need to estimate your operating expenses for the first year after start-up. Chart 4 is used for this estimation.

The first step in determining your annual expenses is to estimate your sales volume month by month. Be sure to consider seasonal treads that may affect your business when estimating the sales volume. Information on seasonal sales patters and typical operating ratios can be secured from your trade association.

(Note: The relationship between the amount of capital that you invest, the level of sales, each of the cost categories, the number of times that you will sell your inventory (turnover) and many other items form "financial ratios."

These ratios provide you with extremely valuable checkpoints before it's too late to make adjustments. In the reference section of your local library are publications such as "The Almanac of Business and Industrial Financial Ratios," as a source of ratios to compare your performance with that of other, similar businesses.

Next determine the cost of goods that will be sold to produce your expected sales. The cost of goods sold or the operating ratios is expressed in dollars and as percentages of sales.

After determining the operating ratios, estimate the expenses necessary to achieve your anticipated sales.

As you prepare Chart 4, understand that you are looking for the percent of total sales that each item represents. Fill out each month's column in dollars, total them in the far right column, and then divide each item into the total net sales to produce the operating ratios. Now fill in Chart 4.

PROJECTED PROFIT/LOSS

	%	I	F	M	A	M	I	I	A	S	O	N	D	Total
Total net Sales														
Cost, goods sold														
Gross														
Controllable expense														
Salaries/wages														
Payroll taxes														
Legal/Accounting														
Advertising														
Automobile														
Office supplies														
Dues/Subscriptions														
Telephone														
Utilities														
Miscellaneous														
Total Con. Exp.														
Fixed Expenses														

	%	J	F	M	A	M	J	J	A	S	O	N	D	Total
Rent														
Depreciation														
Insurance														
Licenses/Permits														
Taxes														
Loan Payments														
Total Fixed Exp.														
Total Expenses														
Net profit/Loss (before tax)														

AFTER START-UP

The primary source of revenue in your business will be from sales but your sales will vary from month to month because of seasonal patterns and other factors. So it is important to determine if your monthly sales will produce enough income to pay each month's bills.

An estimated cash flow projection (Chart 5) will show if the monthly cash balance is going to subject to such factors as:

  – failure to recognize seasonal trends.
  – Excessive cash taken from the business for living expenses;
  – Too rapid expansion, and
  – Slow collection of accounts if credit is extended to customers.

Use the following to build a worksheet to help you with this problem. In this example, all sales made for cash.

Chart 5
ESTIMATED CASH FLOW FORECAST

	Jan	Feb	Mar	Apr	May	Jun	Jul	Aug	(etc.)
Cash in bank (1st of MO.)									
Petty Cash (1st of MO.)									

	Jan	Feb	Mar	Apr	May	Jun	Jul	Aug	(etc.)
Total cash (1st of MO.)									
Anticipated Cash sales									
Total									
Total cash and Receipts									
Disbursements For month Rent, loan Payments Utilities Wages, etc.									
Cash Balance (End of Month)									

CONCLUSION

Beyond a doubt, preparing an adequate business plan is the most important step in starting a new business. A comprehensive business plan will be your guide to managing a successful business. The Business plan is paramount to your success. It must contain all the pertinent information about your business; it must be well written, factual, and organized in a logical sequence. Moreover, it should not contain any statement that cannot be supported.

If you have carefully answered all the questions on this checklist and completed all the worksheets, you have seriously thought about your goal. But there may be some things you feel you need to know more about.

Owning and running a business is a continuous learning process. Research you idea and do as much as you can yourself, but don't hesitate to seek help from people who can tell you what you need to know.

The business plan is your company's principal sales tool in raising capital. Before risking any capital, investors want to reassure themselves that you have thought through your plans carefully, and that you know what you are doing, and that you can respond effectively to problems and opportunities.

They will insist on seeing your business plan before considering any investment, and often will not even meet with entrepreneurs without a prior review of the business plan.

Therefore, your business plan must be well prepared and persuasive in conveying the potential of the company it describes. It should address all major issues, and yet not be so detailed that it "turns off" the investor-reader. You should try not to have a business plan more than 50 pages long.

The guidelines that follow describe:

1. The necessary sections of a business plan;
2. What should be included in each section and subsection?
3. Why the information is necessary and where to find it.

Intelligent use of these guidelines should result in a complete professional business plan which makes an orderly presentation of the facts necessary to obtain an investment decision. Common sense should be used in applying the guidelines to develop a business plan for each venture.

Because the guidelines were written to cover a variety of possible ventures, rigid adherence to them is not possible or even desirable for all ventures. For example, a plan for a service business would not require a discussion of manufacturing nor product design.

STARTING A SMALL BUSINESS

When planning to start a new business, you need to ask yourself:

1. What's in this for me?

_____

_____

_____

2. Why should I spend my time drawing up a business plan?

_____

_____

_____

If you've never drawn up a plan, it is understandable that you want to hear about the possible benefits before you do your work.

A business plan offers at least four benefits. You may find others as you make and use such a plan. The four are:

1. The first, and most important, benefit is that a plan gives you a path to follow. A plan makes the future what you want it to be. A plan with goals and action steps allows you to guide your business through turbulent economic times. It helps the entrepreneur focus ideas.

2. A plan makes it easy to let your banker in on the action. By reading, or hearing, the details of your plan he/she will have real insight into you situation if he/she is to lend you money. It creates a track for management to follow in the early stage of the business.

3. A plan can be a communication tool when you need to orient sales personnel, suppliers, and others about your operations and goals. It creates benchmarks against which the entrepreneur and management can measure progress.

4. A plan can help you develop as a manager. It can give you practice in thinking about competitive conditions, promotional opportunities, and situations that seem to be advantage to your business. Such practice over a period of time can help increase an entrepreneur's ability to make judgments.

WHY AM I IN BUSINESS? _____

_____

_____

_____

_____

Many enterprising Americans are drawn into starting their own business by the possibilities of making money and being their own boss. But the long hours, hard work, and responsibilities of being the boss quickly dispel any preconceived glamour.

Profit is the reward for satisfying consumer needs but it must be worked for. Sometimes a new business might need two years before it show a profit. So where, then, are reasons for having your own business?

BUSINESS PLAN OUTLINE

There are no hard-and-fast rules in formatting a business plan. The length and content often will vary depending on such factors as the company's maturity, the nature and complexity of the business, and the markets it serves. The following format can be effective and comparatively easy to develop.

THE EXECUTIVE SUMMARY

This section is a summary of the key elements of the plan.

The summary is sometimes all the potential investors will read, so it must capture one's attention. An effective summary will properly position the company and help to distinguish your concept from the competition. If the summary fails to move the potential investor into the depth of your plan, it has failed to do its job.

THE EXECUTIVE SUMMARY SHOUD INCLUDE:

- A description of your business, target markets, your product's or service's differentiation from the competition, and why your firm will succeed. This explanation should include information on the size and growth rate of the market for the company's product or service, and a statement indicating the percentage of t that market that will be captured. A brief statement about industry-wide trends is also useful.

- A description of your management team, including their skills, experience and weakness.

- A summary of key financial projections over the next three to five years. You should state your initial and third year sales and profit goals.

- A summary of funding requirements, when the funds will be needed, and how the capital will be spent. You should state your initial and third year sales and profit goals.

- A summary of funding requirements, when the funds will be needed, and how the capital will be spent. You should also state clearly the amount of equity investment you want and any long-term loans that you can obtain.

The executive summary should be a 1-2 page summary of your business plan. It should be brief, appealing and accurate presentation of the highlights of your venture and its opportunities.

1. THE BUSINESS AND ITS INDUSTRY

This section should describe the nature and history of the company and provide some background on its industry. It provides the potential investors with insight that allows them to better understand the projections and estimates presented in subsequent sections.

THE COMPANY

On what date will the venture become a legal entity? _____

_____

_____

Will the business be profit or non-profit? _____

_____

_____

What type of business organization will you be forming? _____

_____

_____

What business am I in? _____

_____

_____

Why is the company being formed? _____

_____

_____

What opportunities do you see for your products, processes or services? _____

_____

_____

DISCUSSION OF INDUSTRY

Present the current status and prospects for the industry in which the proposed business will operate.

What if any new products or developments are in the industry. _____

_____

_____

What new markets are in the industry? _____

_____

_____

What new companies are in the industry? _____

_____

_____

What other trends and factors are in the industry that could affect the venture's business positively or negatively? _____

_____

_____

Identify the source of all information used to describe industry trends. _____

_____

_____

_____

_____

_____

2. THE PRODUCTS OR SERVICES

The potential investor will be vitally interested in exactly what you are doing to sell, what you are going to sell, what kind of product protection you have and the opportunities and possible drawbacks to your product or services.

A. Description: Describe in detail the products or service to be sold.

_____

_____

_____

Discuss the application or function for the products or services you will offer.

_____

_____

_____

Describe the primary end-user of your products or services. _____

_____

_____

Describe any secondary applications for your products or services.

_____

_____

_____

Highlight any product or service differentiation between what is currently on the market and what you will offer, such as lower cost or greater versatility.

_____

_____

_____

Define the present state of development of the product or service. For products, provide a summary or the functional specifications. Include photographs when available.

_____

_____

_____

B. Proprietary Position: Describe in detail any patents, trade secrets or other proprietary features.

_____

_____

_____

_____

Attach copies of any patents applied for or granted. Discuss any head start that you might have that would enable you to achieve a favored or entrenched position.

C. Potential: Describe in detail any features of your product or service that may give it an advantage over the competition.

_____

_____

_____

_____

List any opportunities for the expansion of the product line or the development of related products or services.

_____

_____

_____

_____

List your opportunities and explain how you will take advantage of them.

_____

_____

_____

_____

_____

List any product disadvantages or the possibilities of rapid obsolescence because of technological or styling changes, or marketing fads.

_____

_____

_____

_____

_____

3. MARKET RESEARCH AND EVALUATION

To be an attractive investment, a company should be selling to a market that is large and growing- - where a small market-share can be significant sales volume. The company's competition should be profitable but not so strong as to overwhelm you.

The purpose of this section is to present sufficient facts to convince the reader that the product or service has a substantial market and can achieve sales in the face of competition.

A. Customers: Who are the customers for the anticipated product or service?

_____

_____

_____

_____

Classify potential customers into relatively homogeneous groups (major market segment) having common identifiable characteristics.

What are the population and its growth potential for potential customers?

_____

_____

_____

What is the median income for potential customers? _____

_____

_____

What is the average age of potential customers? _____

_____

_____

What is the typical occupation of potential customers?_____

_____

_____

What is the number of competitive services in and around your proposed location?

_____

_____

_____

What are the local ordinances and zoning regulations?

_____

_____

_____

In what type of trading area are you located?

Commercial? _____

_____

Industrial _____

_____

Residential _____

_____

Who and where are the major purchasers for the product or service in each market segment?

_____

_____

_____

What are the bases of their purchase decisions: price, quality, services, personal contact, and political pressures?

_____

_____

_____

List any potential customers who have expressed an interest in the product or service and indicate why.

_____

_____

_____

_____

_____

List any potential customers who have shown no interest in the proposed product or service and explain why this is so.

_____

_____

_____

_____

_____

Explain what you will do to overcome negative customer reaction.

_____

_____

_____

_____

_____

B. Market Size and Trends: What is the size of the current total market for the product or service offered? The market size should be determined from available data on the purchase of potential customers in each major market segment.

_____

_____

_____

Describe the size of the total market in both units and dollars.

_____

_____

_____

_____

If you intend to sell regionally, show the regional market size.

_____

_____

_____

Indicate the source of data and methods used to establish current market size. Also state the credentials of people doing market research.

_____

_____

_____

Describe the potential annual growth of the total market for your product or service for each customer group. Total market projections should be made for at least three future years.

_____

_____

_____

_____

_____

Discuss the major factors affecting market growth (industry trends, socio-economic trends, government policy, population shifts) and review previous trends in the market.

_____

_____

_____

_____

_____

Explain any differences between past and projected annual growth rates.

_____

_____

_____

List the sources of all data and methods used to make projections.

_____

_____

_____

C. Competition: Make a realistic assessment of the strengths and weaknesses of competitive products and services and name the companies that supply them. State data sources used to determine products and strengths of competition.

Strengths of competitive products and services _____

_____

_____

Weaknesses of competitive products and services _____

_____

_____

State data source used to determine products and strengths of competition.

Compare competing products or services on the basis of price, performance, service warranty and other pertinent features.

_____

_____

_____

_____

Present a short discussion of the current advantages and disadvantages of competing products and say why they are not meeting customers' needs.

_____

_____

_____

Indicate any knowledge of competitors' actions that could lead you to new or improved products and advantageous positions. _____

_____

_____

List the strengths and weaknesses of the competing companies.

_____

_____

_____

Determine and discuss the market share of each competitor—company its sales, distribution and production capabilities._____

_____

_____

List the profitability of the competition and their profit trends.

_____

_____

_____

Who is the pricing leader? _____

_____

_____

Who is the quality leader? _____

_____

_____

Discuss why any companies have entered or dropped out of the market in recent years.

_____

_____

_____

Indicate any knowledge of competitors' actions that could lead you to new or improved products and advantageous positions.

_____

_____

_____

List the strengths and weaknesses of the competing companies. _____

_____

_____

Determine and discuss the market share of each competitor—company, its sales, distribution and production capabilities._____

_____

_____

List the profitability of the competition and their profit trends.

_____

_____

_____

Who is the pricing leader? _____

_____

_____

Who is the quality leader? _____

_____

_____

Discuss why any companies have entered or dropped out of the market in recent years.

_____

_____

_____

List your three or four key competitors and why the customers buy from them.

_____

_____

_____

_____

From what you know about their operations, explain why you think that you can capture a share of their business.

_____

_____

_____

_____

List what makes you think it will be easy or difficult to compete with them.

Easy _____

_____

_____

Difficult _____

_____

_____

D. Estimate Market Share and Sales: List what it is about your product or service that will make it saleable in the face of current and potential competition.

_____

_____

_____

_____

_____

_____

Identify any major first-year customers who are willing to make purchase commitments

_____

_____

_____

Indicate the extent of those commitments and why they were made.

_____

_____

_____

List which customers could be major purchasers in subsequent years and why.

_____

_____

_____

<u>Based on your assessment:</u> List the advantages of your product or service.

_____

_____

_____

List the market size and trends. _____

_____

_____

List the customers for your product or service. _____

_____

_____

List the competition and their product or service. _____

_____

_____

List the share of the market that you will acquire in each of the next three years.

_____

_____

_____

The growth of the company sales and its estimated market share should be related to the growth of its industry and customers and the strengths and weakness of competitors.

The data can best be presented in tabular form. The assumptions used to estimate market share and sales should be clearly stated.

E. <u>Ongoing Market Evaluation:</u> Explain how you will continue to evaluate your target markets so as to: assess customer needs and guide product improvement programs and new-product programs: plan for expansions of; your production facility: and guide product/service pricing.

_____

_____

_____

_____

4. MARKETING PLAN

A marketing plan is one of the most important aspects of any small business. It will assist in evaluating your company's marketing needs and give you a concise direction in your marketing efforts. Above all, if developed properly, the plan should help you increase your market share in a cost—effective, timely and productive manner. Marketing plans only work if you implement them – writing them is just the first step.

The marketing plan should include:

A. The philosophy of the company.
Define what the company does and the product or service it is marketing. Evaluate what the company is trying to do internally and externally.

_____

_____

_____

_____

B. You're marketing goals.
Include short-and long-term goals. Most companies have a number of marketing goals that need to be addressed. When determining these goals it is important to prioritize them in order of need and availability of funds. Consider the following questions:

Do you want to introduce a new product or service to the marketplace?

_____

_____

_____

Do you need to increase your existing market share? _____

_____

_____

Do you need to create a new image? Revise the existing image?

_____

_____

_____

Do you need to increase your sales or new business by a certain percentage?

_____

_____

_____

Do you want to expand your target audience or approach new audiences?

_____

_____

_____

Do you need to educate your audience or just sell to them? _____

_____

_____

C. Establish a budget – and stick to it.

A budget should be created for a minimum of 12 months. The key to a successful budget is to be realistic, be patient concerning the results and, above all be willing to spend the money allotted to the budget.

_____

_____

_____

D. Create a timeline to accomplish the marketing goals.

_____

_____

_____

E. Create a strategic plan to implement the marketing goals.

Make sure your strategies are consistent with the budget and the timeline. Consider the following questions:

Is advertising the best use of your budget? _____

_____

_____

Will it reach the target audience or would direct marketing be more effective?

_____

_____

_____

If you do advertise, can you afford to do so consistently? If no, don't do it.

_____

_____

_____

Would a simple brochure relay your message? _____

_____

_____

Could you distribute it effectively? _____

_____

_____

Would low-cost advertising such as coupon books, inserts and flyers get your name out in the community?

_____

_____

_____

Do you need to educate the audience with your efforts or just sell to them?

_____

_____

_____

What kind of "call to action" would you utilize?

_____

_____

_____

Are public relations an avenue to consider?

_____

_____

_____

F. Develop an effective team to implement these strategies.
Most small businesses don't have the time and resources to implement the strategies. Contact experts to assist, such as freelance graphic designers and writers, media and research consultants, advertising agencies and experienced individuals in your company.

_____

_____

_____

G. Devise an approach to track your efforts.
Review the budget, the marketing media you are using, and the results. Know what is working and what needs to be revised and keep a record of it. _____

_____

_____

H. Develop the marketing plan for next year based on results.

_____

_____

_____

5. MARKET RESEARCH

Whether or not there is a demand for your business may be hard to assess. To reduce the risk of starting a new business, you can do market research. Although research cannot guarantee success in your business, it can improve your chances by estimating sales potential and avoiding losses caused by lack of market demand. Before investing your time and money in a market research study, however, there are a number of things you should consider:

Qualify the needs of the marketplace (determine what the customer wants).

_____

_____

_____

Who will purchase the product or services? _____

_____

_____

Who makes the buying decisions? _____

_____

_____

What is the current demand? _____

_____

_____

How many companies providing those products or services currently satisfy that demand?

_____

_____

_____

When is the product purchased?_____

_____

_____

Why?_____

_____

_____

Is it seasonal? _____

_____

_____

Where is the product purchased and where is the buying decision made?

_____

_____

_____

How does the potential customer buy the product now?

_____

_____

_____

Will that customer buy the product again, and how is it financed or serviced?

_____

_____

_____

Indicate whether the product or service will initially be introduced nationally or on a regional level.

_____

_____

_____

Describe any plans to obtain government contracts as means of supporting manufacturing or product-development costs and overhead.

_____

_____

_____

_____

<u>What you must know to do your own market analysis</u>
Know your product.

What need will it satisfy?

_____

_____

_____

How good is it relative to the competition?

_____

_____

_____

Is it priced fairly?

_____

_____

_____

Try to determine the quality and quantity of your market segment. For example, in the retail business, it would be helpful to know the average income of the people in your selling area to predict spending levels and to estimate how many people are potential customers. Obtain other demographic information, things like size of industry which are useful in estimating market potential.

_____

_____

_____

_____

_____

Determine the proper location for your business. Gather information about traffic patterns (vehicular and pedestrian) to assess sales potential. The Department of Highways Division of Transportation Planning has information on vehicular movement and can provide traffic volume maps which show area volume on an average day. Observe pedestrian movement during business hours to estimate pedestrian numbers.

_____

_____

_____

_____

_____

You will want to consider the following list of questions in picking the specific site for your business.

Will the customer come to your place of business?

_____

_____

_____

How much space do you need?

_____

_____

_____

Will you want to expand later on?

_____

_____

_____

Do you need any special features required in lighting, heating, and ventilation?

_____

_____

_____

Is parking available? _____

_____

_____

Is public transportation available? _____

_____

_____

Is the location conductive to drop-in customers? _____

_____

_____

Will you pick up and deliver? _____

_____

_____

Will travel time be expensive? _____

_____

_____

Will you prorate travel time to service calls? _____

_____

_____

Would a location close to an expressway or main artery cut down on travel time?

_____

_____

_____

If you choose a remote location, will savings in rent offset the inconvenience?

_____

_____

_____

If you choose a remote location, will you have to pay as much as you save in rent for advertising to make your service known?_____

_____

_____

If you choose a remote location, will the customer be able to readily locate your business?

_____

_____

_____

Will the supply of labor be adequate and the necessary skills available?

_____

_____

_____

What are the zoning regulations of the area? _____

_____

_____

Will there be adequate fire and police protection? _____

_____

_____

Will crime insurance be needed and available at a reasonable rate?

_____

_____

_____

I plan to locate "my business at" _____

_____

_____

Is the area in which you plan to locate supported by a strong economic base? For example, are nearby industries working full time? Only part time? Did any industries close in the past several months? _____

_____

_____

Are new industries scheduled to open in the nest several months?

_____

_____

_____

Write your opinion of the area's economic base and your reason for that opinion here.

_____

_____

_____

Will you build?

_____

_____

_____

What are the terms of the loan or mortgage?

_____

_____

_____

Will you rent? _____ What are the terms of the lease? _____

_____

_____

_____

Is the building attractive? _____ In good repair? _____

_____

_____

_____

_____

_____

Will it need remodeling?

_____

_____

_____

Cost of remodeling $ _____ What services does the landlord provide?

_____

_____

_____

What is the competition in the geographic area you have picked?

_____

_____

_____

The number of firms that handle my services or product.

_____

_____

_____

Does the area appear to be saturated? _____

_____

_____

How many of these firms look prosperous?

_____

_____

_____

Do they have any advantages over you? _____

_____

_____

How many look as though they're barely getting by?

_____

_____

_____

How many similar services went out of business in this area last year?

_____

_____

_____

Can you find out why they failed? _____

_____

_____

How many new services opened up in the last year?

_____

_____

_____

Which firm or firms in the area will be your biggest competition?

_____

_____

_____

List the reasons for your opinion here. _____

_____

_____

When you have a location in mind, you should work through another aspect of marketing. How will you attract customers to your business?

_____

_____

_____

How will you pull customers away from you competition?

_____

_____

_____

Check the local Yellow Pages to find out who your major competitors are.

_____

_____

_____

Doing a market study/
If you want to hire someone to conduct your research, private firms offer full or partial services and will perform an extensive market study including design, administration and analysis. Fees will vary depending upon the study; Consult your Yellow Pages for listings.

_____

_____

_____

_____

_____

_____

If you want to do your own research, the following list, though not exhausting, will serve as a general guide to sources offering market research information at little or no cost to the individual.

U. S. DEPARTMENT OF COMMERCE CENSUS BUREAU – The Census Bureau offers statistical profiles of the area and general social and economic characteristics such as population composition, age, income, education and industry of employed persons.

_____

_____

_____

U. S. SMALL BUSINESS ADMINISTRATION – The SBA offers a wide variety of services on market research.

_____

_____

_____

DEPARTMENT OF LABOR AND EMPLOYMENT/DIVISION OF EMPLOYMENT AND TRANING –The Department's Labor Market Information Section provides demographic breakdowns; publishes a "State Labor Market Information Directory" and an Annual Planning Information Report," covering the state and local labor market areas.

_____

_____

_____

_____

DEPARTMENT OF EMPLOYMENT LABOR MARKET INFORMATION

_____

_____

_____

CHAMBER OF COMMERCE – Your local chamber can provide business development and real estate information and various municipal facts.

_____

_____

_____

_____

TRADE ASSOCIATIONS – Trade Associations may be useful to help you find out the number of similar merchants in your market and may also assist you with information to get started. You can find listings in the reference sections of the public library under the "Encyclopedia of Associations".

_____

_____

_____

_____

PUBLIC LIBRARIES – The library provides access and assistance to help you research more than 1,000,000 publications by federal, state and local government agencies and also has a business periodicals index.

_____

_____

_____

UNIVERSITIES AND COMMUNITY COLLEGES – Universities are a good source of information. Business school departments may offer student market studies for no charge and professors may charge a modest fee. Also, extensive library collections may be available for public use.

_____

_____

_____

6. PRICING

The pricing policy is one of the more important decisions you will have to make. The "price must be right" to penetrate the market, maintain a market position and produce profits.

Discuss the prices to be charged for your product or service and compare your pricing policy with those of your major competitors.

_____

_____

_____

Discuss the gross profit margin between manufacturing and ultimate sales costs.

_____

_____

_____

How will the price get the product or service accepted?

_____

_____

_____

How will the price help you maintain and desirably increase your market share in the face of competition? _____

_____

_____

How will the price help you produce profit?

_____

_____

_____

Justify any price increases over competitive items on the basis of newness, quality, warranty and service. If a lower price is to be charges, explain how you will do this and maintain profitability- e.g., greater effectiveness in manufacturing and distributing the product, lower labor costs, lower overhead, or lower material cost.

_____

_____

_____

_____

_____

List the relationship of price, market share and profit. For example, a higher price may reduce volume but result in higher gross profit.

_____

_____

_____

_____

_____

List any discount allowance for prompt payment or volume purchase.

_____

_____

_____

_____

_____

a. <u>Sales Tactics:</u> Describe the methods that will be used to make sales and distribute the product or service.

Will the company use its own sales force? _____

_____

_____

Will the company use its own sales representatives?

_____

_____

_____

Will the company use a distributor? _____

_____

_____

Are there ready-made manufacturers' organizations already selling related products that can be used?

_____

_____

_____

Describe both the initial plans and longer range plans for a sales force.

_____

_____

_____

_____

_____

If distributors or sales representatives are to be used, describe how they have been selected._____

_____

_____

When will they start to represent you and the areas they will cover?

_____

_____

_____

_____

_____

Show a table that indicates the build-up of dealers and representatives by month and the expected sales to be made by each dealer.

_____

_____

_____

_____

_____

Describe any special policies regarding discounts, exclusive distribution rights, etc.

_____

_____

_____

_____

_____

If a direct sales force is to be used, indicate how it will be structured and at what rate it will be built up.

_____

_____

_____

_____

If it is to replace a dealer or representative organization indicate when and how.

_____

_____

_____

_____

Show the sales expected per salesperson per year, and what commission incentive and/or salary reach is slated to receive.

_____

_____

_____

_____

If OEM (original equipment manufacturer) or government contacts are expected or essential, discuss how, why and when these will be obtained.

_____

_____

_____

_____

Present, as an exhibit, a selling schedule and a sales budget that includes all marketing, promotion and service costs. This sales expense exhibit should also indicate when sales will commence and the lapse between a sale and a delivery.

_____

_____

_____

_____

_____

_____

_____

_____

_____

_____

D. <u>Service and Warranty Policies:</u> If your company will offer a product requiring service and warranties, indicate the importance of these to the customers' purchasing decision and discuss your method of handling service problems.

Describe the kind and terms of any warranties to be offered, and whether service will be handled by company service people, agencies, dealers and distributors.

_____

_____

_____

_____

_____

Indicate the proposed charge for service calls and whether service will be profitable or break even operation.

_____

_____

_____

_____

_____

Compare your service and warranty policies and practices with those of your principal competitors and indicate what kind of service manual will be prepared.

_____

_____

_____

_____

_____

E. Advertising and Promotion: Describe the approaches the company will use to bring its product to the attention of prospective purchasers.

_____

_____

_____

For OEM and industrial products indicate the plans for trade-show participation, trade magazine advertisements, direct-mailings, the preparation of product sheets and promotional literature, and use of advertising agencies.

_____

_____

_____

For consumer products, indicate what kind of advertising and promotional campaign is contemplated to introduce the product and what kind of sales-aids will be provided to dealers.

_____

_____

_____

The schedule and cost of promotion and advertising should be presented. If advertising will be a significant part of company expenses, an exhibit showing how and when these costs will be incurred should be included.

_____

_____

_____

_____

7. DESIGN AND DEVELOPMENT PLANS

If the product, process or service or the proposed venture requires any design and development before it is ready to be placed on the market, the nature and extent of this work should be fully discussed.

_____

_____

_____

_____

_____

_____

The investor will want to know the extent and nature of any design and development and the costs and time required to achieve a marketable product. Such design and development might be the engineering work necessary to convert a laboratory prototype to a finished product; the design of special tooling; the work of an industrial designer to make a product more attractive and saleable; or the identification and organization of manpower. Equipment and special techniques to implement and service business - e.g. the equipment, new computer software and skills required for computerized credit-checking.

_____

_____

_____

_____

_____

_____

_____

_____

A. Development Status and Tasks: Describe the current status of the product or service and explain what remains to be done to make it marketable.

_____

_____

_____

_____

_____

Describe, briefly, the competence or expertise that your company has or can acquire to complete this development. Indicate the type and extent of technical assistance that will be required, state who will supervise this activity within your organization and his/her experience in related development work.

_____

_____

_____

_____

_____

_____

_____

_____

_____

_____

B. Difficulties and Risks: Identify any major anticipated design and development problems and approaches to their solution.

_____

_____

_____

_____

_____

Discuss their possible effect on the schedule and cost of design and development and time of market introduction.

_____

_____

_____

_____

_____

_____

_____

C. Product Improvement and New Products: In addition to describing the development of the initial products, discuss any ongoing design and development work that is planned to keep your product or service competitive and develop new related products that can be sold to the same group of customers.

_____

_____

_____

_____

_____

_____

_____

D. <u>Costs:</u> Present and discuss a design and development budget. The costs should include labor, materials consulting fees, etc. Miscalculations are often made about design and development costs and this can seriously impact cash-flow projections. Accordingly, consider and perhaps show a 10-20% cost contingency. These cost data will become an integral part of the financial plan.

_____

_____

_____

_____

_____

_____

_____

_____

_____

8. MANUFACTURING AND OPERATIONS PLAN

The manufacturing and operations plan should describe the kind of facilities, plant location, space requirements, capital equipment and labor force (part or full-time) required to product the company's product or service.

_____

_____

_____

_____

_____

For a manufacturing business, stress should also be given to the production process that will be used; inventory control, purchasing and production control: and to "make or buy decisions", i. e., which operations will be performed by your work force.

_____

_____

_____

A service business may require particular attention to and focus on an appropriate location, an ability to minimize overhead, leasing the required equipment, and obtaining competitive productivity from a skilled or trained labor force.

_____

_____

_____

The discussion guidelines given below are general enough to cover both product and service businesses. Only those that are relevant to your venture – be it product or service – should be addressed in the business plan.

1. Geographic Location: Describe the planned geographical location of the business and discuss any advantages or disadvantages of the site location in terms of wage rates, labor unions, labor availability, transportation, state and local tax laws, utilities and zoning regulations. For a service business, proximity to customers is a "must."

_____

_____

_____

_____

_____

_____

_____

Describe how your propose to overcome any problems associated with the location.

_____

_____

_____

_____

_____

_____

_____

2. <u>Facilities and Improvements:</u> Describe the facilities required to start and conduct the company's business.

_____

_____

_____

_____

_____

Indicate the requirements for plant and office space, storage and land areas, machinery, special tools and other capital equipment and utilities.

_____

_____

_____

_____

Discuss any facilities currently owned or leased that could be used for the proposed venture.

_____

_____

_____

_____

_____

Describe how initial plan space and equipment will be expanded to reach the capacity required by future sales projections. Indicate the timing and costs of such expansion are acquisitions. A three-year planning period should be used for these projections.

_____

_____

_____

_____

_____

Discuss any plans to improve or add to existing plant space or to move the facility.

_____

_____

_____

_____

_____

3. <u>Strategy and Plans:</u> Describe the manufacturing processes involved in your product's production and any decisions in respect to subcontracting of component parts rather than complete in-house manufacture. The "make or buy" strategy adopted should be determined by inventory financing, available skilled labor and other non-technical questions as well as production, cost and capability issues (your company might operate as a labor-intensive assembly plant or purchase basic parts and subassemblies).

_____

_____

_____

_____

_____

Justify your proposed "make or buy" policy.

_____

_____

_____

_____

Discuss any surveys of potential subcontractors and suppliers, what is likely to be their contribution, and terms and conditions applying to paying for inventory.

_____

_____

_____

_____

_____

Present a production or operations plan that show cost and various levels of operations with a full break-down of applicable material, labor, purchased components and factory burden.

_____

_____

_____

_____

_____

Discuss the inventory required at various sales levels. This data will be incorporated into cash-flow projections. The operations plan should also discuss build-up in the labor force and relate the added labor hours to increased output.

_____

_____

_____

_____

_____

Explain how any seasonal production loads will be handled without severe disruption, e.g., by building in inventory or part-time help in peak periods. If there are daily shift-to-shift variations in the labor force (for a service business) discuss them and how they will be handled.

_____

_____

_____

_____

_____

Briefly, describe your approach to quality control, production control, and inventory control. Explain what quality control and inspection procedures the company will use to minimize service problems and associated customer dissatisfaction.

_____

_____

_____

_____

_____

_____

_____

_____

Discuss how you will organize and operate your purchasing function to ensure that adequate materials are on had for production, which the best price has been obtained for raw materials and in-process inventory, thus maximizing, working capital.

_____

_____

_____

_____

_____

_____

_____

4. <u>Labor Force:</u> Exclusive of management functions (discussed later), does the local labor force have the necessary skills in sufficient quantity and quality (lack of absenteeism, productivity), to manufacture the product or supply the services of the proposed company? If the skills of the labor force are inadequate for the needs of the company, describe the kinds of training you will use to upgrade their skills.

_____

_____

_____

_____

_____

_____

Discuss whether the new business can offer such training and still offer a competitive product both in the short term (first year) and longer term (2-5 years).

_____

_____

_____

_____

_____

_____

_____

9. MANAGEMENT TEAM

Lack of management expertise or experience, is apparent, especially to most business plan inventors. The management team is the key to investors who will supply the capital to start the company, so it is important that this deficiency be overcome if the start-up business is to be financed and managed in a successful manner. Investors look for a committed management team with a proper balance of technical, managerial and business skills and experience in doing what is proposed.

Accordingly, this section of the business plan will be of primary interest to potential investors and will significantly influence their investment decisions. I should include a description of the key management personnel and their primary duties in the organizational structure, and an introduction of the board of directors.

_____

_____

_____

_____

_____

_____

A. <u>ORGANIZATION:</u> Present in tabular form the key management roles in the company and the individuals who will fill each position.

_____

_____

_____

_____

_____

_____

Discuss any prior experience in working together this indicates how skills complement each other and result in an effective management team.

If any key individuals will not be on board at the beginning of the venture, indicate when they will join the company.

_____

_____

_____

_____

_____

_____

_____

_____

_____

_____

In a new business, it may not be possible to fill each executive role with a full-time person without excessively burdening the overhead of the venture. One solution is to use part-time specialists or consultants to perform some functions. If this is your plan, discuss it and indicate who will fill in and when these individuals will be replaced by a full-time staff member. Therefore, many small businesses may choose to use external professional service advisors, such as accountants, attorneys, technical consultants, management consultants and others.

Some advisors, primarily accountants and attorneys, are widely used by businesses of all sizes because of regulatory and legal requirements. No business can function without maintaining financial records, filing required reports, paying income and other taxes, or keeping a financial record for use in dealing with banks, suppliers, or others who need to know the financial positions of the organization. By the same token, most businesses have need of legal advice regarding company structure, contractual arrangements with suppliers and distributors, leases, liability protection against litigation, etc.

While this makes the use of accountants and attorneys in small businesses more common than other professional advisors, their broad usage does not diminish the need to select those advisors any less carefully. All advisors should be chosen with great care, including adequate credential and reference checking. Engineers, technical specialists, management consultants, and others who provide, highly specialized advice should be screened just as carefully. In addition, the specific expertise that they can bring to a situation must also be verified to determine if it is correct for the need. If you decide you need an advisor, the following steps will help you.

Define what type/kind of advice you think you need; general (e.g. legal, accounting, etc) or specific (e.g. sales contracts, audit, marketing plan, etc.) Put those thoughts on paper to help define and clarify you thinking and shorten your search time and ultimate cost.

_____

_____

_____

Make a list of potential advisors that you could use. Ask business associates and friends. Ask your business associates and friends. Ask your business or industry association. Ask you current advisor (lawyer, accountant, banker, and consultant) about other advisors. Ask local professional associations trade organizations or chambers of commerce for referrals.

_____

_____

_____

Screen your list to determine (for each): if they regularly provide the specific help you need are their experiences in similar situations.

_____

_____

_____

_____

_____

How long have they been practicing?

_____

_____

_____

What professional certification have they achieved?

_____

_____

_____

What references can they provide from clients?

_____

_____

_____

What do they charge and how?

_____

_____

_____

How much time would be required to handle your project?

_____

_____

_____

When would they be free to do your work? _____

_____

_____

Do they appear to be knowledgeable about, empathetic with, and understanding of your needs? (This later screening is better done via personal visit, whereas the prior information can generally be secured by telephone).

Confirm the potential advisors' experience and check references. Then make your selection based on the following:

Breadth of experience and professional credentials. _____

_____

_____

Ability to complete assignments on time, within, budget.

_____

_____

_____

Ability to develop practical and workable solutions and recommendations.

_____

_____

_____

Demonstrated ability to work effectively within organizations without interrupting the ongoing business or alienating employees.

_____

_____

_____

The rapport and trust developed between you and the potential advisor during your telephone and personal interview.

_____

_____

_____

Ask the selected professional advisor to submit a written proposal outlining:

Objectives scope of the assignment.

_____

_____

_____

Nature and form of final report / documents / system (as appropriate) and the timing and format or progress reports as the work proceeds.

_____

_____

_____

Synopsis of what the advisor will do; what the business will do; what you'll do jointly; and how the advisor will proceed with his/her work during the assignment.

_____

_____

_____

Anticipated cost of the project. (fees, expenses); the basis for charges; and the terms of payment. _____

_____

_____

Conditions under which you and/or the advisor may cancel the agreement or contract and any resulting liabilities or restrictions on each side in such cases.

_____

_____

_____

Review the proposal with the advisor and resolve all questions and ambiguities before agreeing to proceed or before signing any contract or other document.

_____

_____

_____

Cooperate with the advisor as work proceeds:

Inform all people involved and allay anxieties to ensure cooperation of all in your organization. _____

_____

_____

Don't try to short circuit the work or shorten the time frame agreed to when the work started, but do insist it be complete on time.

_____

_____

_____

Review the finished work/project and ask yourself:

Did I get what I paid for? (i.e. a system, a document savings, a procedure, improved attitudes, etc.) _____

_____

_____

Obviously some types of advisory work can be evaluated much more easily and readily than others. An accountant dealing with financial statements, audits, or other detailed work may require a longer period of time than someone working on a short-term project such as a contract, lease, or other document. However, evaluated over time all advisory work can and must be if you want to ensure effective use of your dollars and the benefit to your business organization.

Considering everything that happened during the assignment and the product produced, would I hire this advisor again?

_____

_____

_____

_____

_____

_____

_____

If the answer is yes, you've had a successful experience with an advisor. If the answer is no, you need to determine why. You've learned some valuable lessons for future reference and these should be documented now to prevent another unsuccessful experience in the future.

_____

_____

_____

_____

_____

_____

Choosing and using professional advisors is critical to businesses of all sizes and typed and you must select your advisors carefully. A good working relationship with a professional advisor can help your develop a disciplined approach to business problems and improve the chances of reaching your long-term financial goals. In many cases, experienced advisors can assist the entrepreneur with contacts in banks, venture capital firms or other lending sources. Such effective working relationships with outside advisors can give the entrepreneur a wealth of experience, insight, and contacts that can greatly enhance the probability of success.

_____

_____

_____

B. Key Management personnel: Describe the exact duties and responsibilities of each of the key members of the management team. Include a brief (three or four sentence) statement of the career highlights of each individual that focuses on accomplishments demonstrating his/her ability to perform a job or task assigned.

_____

_____

_____

_____

Complete resumes for each key management person should be included as an exhibit to the business plan. These resumes should stress the training, experience, and accomplishments of each member, in performing functions similar to his/her duties in the venture. Accomplishments should be discussed is such concrete manufacturing terms as: profit improvement; labor management; manufacturing or technical achievements; ability to meet budgets and schedules; community organization. Where possible it should be noted who can attest to accomplishments and what recognition or rewards were received – e.g. pay increases, promotions, etc.

_____

_____

_____

_____

C. <u>Management Compensation and Ownership:</u> The likelihood of obtaining financing is small when the founding management team is not prepared to accept initial modest salaries. If the founders demand substantial salaries, potential investors will conclude that their psychological commitment to the venture is less than it should be.

State the salary that is to be paid to each key person and compare it to the salary received at his/her last independent job. Set forth the stock ownership planned for the key personnel, the amount of their equity investment (if any), and any performance-dependent stock-option or bonus plans that are contemplated.

_____

_____

_____

_____

_____

_____

_____

_____

_____

_____

_____

_____

_____

_____

D. <u>Board of Directors:</u> By establishing an effective Board of Directors, the management team can obtain: (1) the participation of local residents to ensure that the business is properly responsive to community needs and effectively taps local resources; and

(2) advice and assistance in dealing with customers and suppliers. Discuss the company's philosophy regarding the size and composition of the board.

Identify proposed board members and include a one-or two-sentence statement of the members' backgrounds showing what each person can bring to the company. A resume for each board member should be included as an Appendix to the business plan.

_____

_____

_____

_____

_____

_____

_____

_____

_____

_____

_____

_____

_____

_____

E. <u>Management Assistance and Training Needs:</u> Describe candidly, the strengths and weaknesses of your management team and the board of directors.

_____

_____

_____

_____

_____

Discuss the type, extent and timing of any management training that will be required to overcome weaknesses and obtain effective business operations.

_____

_____

_____

_____

_____

Discuss also the need for technical and management assistance during the first three years of your venture. Be as specific as you can as to the kind, extent and cost of such assistance and how it be obtained.

_____

_____

_____

_____

_____

F. Supporting Professional Services: State the legal (including patient), accounting advertising and banking organizations that you have selected for your venture. Capable, reputable and well-known supporting service organizations can not only provide significant direct, professional assistance, but can also add to the credibility of your venture. In addition, properly selected professional organizations can help you identify potential investors and help you secure financing.

_____

_____

_____

_____

_____

_____

_____

_____

_____

_____

_____

_____

_____

_____

_____

10.   OVERHALL SCHEDULE

A schedule that shows the timing and interrelationship of the major events necessary to launch the venture and realize its objectives is an essential part of the business plan. In addition to being a planning aid and showing deadlines critical to a venture's success, a well-prepared schedule can be an extremely effective sales tool in raising money form potential investors. Properly prepared and realistic, it demonstrates the ability of the management team to plan for venture growth in a way that recognizes obstacles and minimizes investor risk.

_____

_____

_____

_____

_____

_____

_____

_____

_____

_____

_____

_____

_____

Prepare, as a part of this section, a month-by-month schedule that shows the timing of such activities as: product development; market planning; sales programs; and production and operations. Show the timing of the primary tasks required to accomplish an activity.

Show, on the schedule, the deadlines or milestones critical to the venture's success. These should include events such as:

Incorporation of the venture _____

_____

_____

Completion of design and development _____

_____

_____

Completion of prototypes (a key date; its achievement is a tangible measure of the company's ability to perform) _____

_____

_____

Product display at trade shows _____

_____

_____

Ordering of materials in production quantities _____

_____

_____

Start of production or operation (another key date because it is related to the production of income) _____

_____

_____

First orders received _____

_____

_____

First sales and deliveries (a date of maximum interest because it relates directly to the company's credibility and need for capital)

_____

_____

_____

Payment of first accounts receivable (cash in)

_____

_____

_____

The schedule should also show the following and their relation to the development of the business:

Number of management personnel _____

_____

_____

Number of production and operation personnel _____

_____

_____

Additions to plant or equipment _____

_____

_____

Discuss, in a general way, the activities most likely to cause a schedule delays, and what steps you would take to correct such delays.

_____

_____

_____

Discuss the impact of schedule delays on the venture's operation – especially its potential viability and capital needs. Keep in mind that the time to do things tends to be underestimated – even more than financing requirements. So be realistic about your schedule.

_____

_____

_____

11. CRITICAL RISKS AND ASSUMPTIONS

The development of a business has risks and problems and the business plan invariably contains some implicit assumptions about them. The discovery of any unstated negative factors by potential investors can undermine the credibility of the venture and endanger its financing.

Accordingly, identify and discuss the critical assumptions in the business plan and the major problems that you think you will have to solve to develop the venture. Include a description of the risks and critical assumptions relating to your industry, your company and its personnel, and your product's market appeal and the timing and financing of your start-up.

Among the problem areas that may require discussion are:

Reliability of sales projections – e.g., market does not develop as fast as predicted.

_____

_____

_____

_____

Any potentially unfavorable industry-wide trends

_____

_____

_____

Manufacturing at target costs _____

_____

_____

Ability of competitors to under price or cause your product to become obsolete

_____

_____

_____

Innovation and development required to stay competitive

_____

_____

_____

Meeting the venture-development schedule

_____

_____

_____

Availability of trained labor _____

_____

_____

Procurement of parts or raw materials _____

_____

_____

Need for and timing of initial and additional financing

_____

_____

_____

This list is not meant to be complete but only indicative of the kinds of risks assumptions that might be discussed.

Indicate which business plan assumptions or potential problems are most critical to the success of the venture. Describe your plans for minimizing the impact of unfavorable developments in each area on the success of your venture.

_____

_____

_____

12.   INSURANC NEED – WHAT YOU SHOULD KNOW

Before starting your business, you should look into what types of insurance may be required, or may be in your best interest, to protect your investment, business property and business income. Insurance companies can put together a specialized insurance package to meet the exact needs of your business. While it often makes good business sense to purchase various forms of insurance coverage.

A. General Business Liability

This is the broadest form of coverage which can protect your business against losses when injury, damage or even death results to another person or their property because of business negligence. You may be responsible for obligations covering medical and disability expenses, and even death and funeral compensation, to the dependents of one who has been injured. (Your obligations may even extend beyond the general liability for which you assume you are responsible. Read the terms of the insurance contract carefully).

If you manufacture a product, this type of insurance can also cover the goods you produce. Coverage usually applies once you have given the product to someone else, who will modify or alter it in some way, or distribute it for wholesale or rental sale, Insurance coverage typically relates to the product itself, but may also protect you as the manufactures should someone experience personal injury or property damage from the use of your product.

_____

_____

_____

_____

_____

_____

_____

_____

_____

_____

B. Property Insurance

Property insurance is especially important if you own the property or building where your business is located. As the mortgages, you can be protected against losses and a loss of income in the event your business experiences damage as a result of natural disaster, fire, burglary or vandalism, which may destroy all or part of your property.

_____

_____

_____

C. Specific Time Element Coverage (or Business Interruption Insurance)

Because of personal property damage that might occur to your business from either environmental factors, natural disasters or other destruction, resulting in a loss of business earnings time element coverage can pay for your loss of income until you are able to begin operating again. Reimbursement is only for the amount of actual loss and coverage limits will vary. Limited coverage for a specific amount of time and a specific amount of time and a specific amount of reimbursement (for example for a 30-60-90-or 365-day period, reimbursing you for 50 percent of your profits can help pay for your ongoing business expenses. _____

_____

_____

_____

D. Errors and Omissions/Professional Liability

This form of coverage is often recommended for employees, owners and directors in the business. Errors and omissions and professional liability coverage offers protection for employees and owners of the business against lawsuits that may arise as a result of their actions or failure to act in duties performed during the course of business.

_____

_____

_____

_____

E. Unemployment Insurance and Workers' Compensation

If there are employees in the business, these types of insurance are required by law. This kit can provide you with applications to open these accounts.

_____

_____

_____

_____

F. Bonds

While a bond is not an insurance contract, there are several types of surety bonds businesses can purchase which cover a wide range of losses. Fidelity bonds are designed to protect a business or employer from losses due to the dishonesty of employees, partners or officers in the business. However, the amount of coverage may be limited so you should check with your insurance agent as to the specific amount of coverage necessary. Performance bonds guarantee a business's performance because of an obligation or contractual agreement. If you default on a contract or agreement to do work, a performance bond will guarantee payment to the person who has contracted with you for the remaining work. Different state laws require that certain occupations post a bond before they are awarded a state contract. Bonds usually are not a mandatory requirement; however, many companies do require that you post a bond before beginning work. There are very broad classes of insurance needs which you may want to look into. Since particular business insurance needs can vary, there is not a single, all-inclusive package that can apply to everyone. Again, your business has its own special needs. To best meet the needs of your business, you should consult an insurance agent or broker who is qualified to cover the various options available to you.

_____

_____

_____

_____

_____

_____

_____

_____

_____

_____

_____

13.   LEGAL STRUCTURE – CHOICE OF BUSINESS FORM

All businesses are conducted under some legal form. A business may be conducted in the form of a sole proprietorship, a general partnership, a limited partnership, a limited liability company, or a corporation. There are several issues of particular concern in determining the legal form most suited to the needs of a particular business.

First to what extent will the personal business owner (s) are placed at risk?

_____

_____

_____

_____

_____

Second, who will control the business?

_____

_____

_____

_____

_____

Third how will the business be financed?

_____

_____

_____

_____

Each of the forms of business organization offers advantages and disadvantages. The entrepreneur should examine the characteristics of each of these business forms and determine which is most suited to his or her needs.

A. Sole Proprietorship

A sole proprietorship is a business worked and operated by an individual. There are on formal legal requirements for the establishment of a sole proprietorship; however, if the business is using a tread mane it must be registered with the state.

The primary legal characteristic of the sole proprietorship is that the proprietor is personally liable for all business debts. If the business is unable to meet its financial obligations, its creditors may purse the personal assets of the proprietor. The sole proprietor is generally limited to financing the business by borrowing money. This requires periodic payments to creditors regardless of whether the business is making money. Thus, the fact that the proprietor's personal assets are at risk is an important factor.

All profits and losses of the business pass through and are reported directly on the proprietor's personal income tax return. _____

_____

_____

B. General Partnership

A general partnership is an association of two or more persons organized for the purpose of conducting, as co-owners, a business for profit. There are no formal legal requirements for establishing a general partnership agreement which serves as a legal document between the partners. A partnership is generally financed in two ways; First, Contributions become partnership property and are subject to the claims of the creditors of the business. Second, the partnership can borrow money. Again, this will require the partnership to make periodic payments to the lender regardless of the partnership's ability to pay. All of the partners are jointly and severally liable for the debts of the partnership. Thus, if a general partnership is unable to meet its financial obligations, the personal assets of any one or all of the partners may be attached. _____

_____

_____

_____

_____

_____

C. Limited Partnership

A limited partnership differs from a general partnership in that some partners, i.e., the limited partners, enjoy limited liability. While the general partners remain personally liable for the debts of the partnership, the liability of limited partners is limited to their ownership interest in the partnership. The limited partners play no significant role in the day-to-day operation of control of the business; that role is left to the general partner(s). This gives the limited partnership an additional financing option. The partnership can raise capital by selling interest in the business in the form of limited partnership.

_____

_____

_____

_____

_____

_____

D. Limited Liability Company

A limited liability company is a business structure which combines the concept of a partnership (for tax purposes) and a corporation (for liability purposes). No member of a limited liability company can be sued individually for company acts unless case law would indicate the "corporate Veil" should be pierced. These companies must file Articles of Organization with the Secretary of State's Office on forms provided by that office.

_____

_____

_____

_____

_____

_____

_____

E. Corporation

A corporation is a legal entity owned by its shareholders and run by a board of directors elected by the shareholders. Anyone receiving compensation from the corporation, including working officers, are considered employees for the purpose of state and federal income tax withholding, unemployment insurance, and workers' compensation.

Two primary characteristics distinguish a corporation from other business forms. A corporation is liable for business debts only to the extent of the corporate assets. The shareholders' personal assets are thus completely shielded from the corporation's creditors. Second corporate profits may be subject to double taxation. A corporation must pay tax on its income just like an ordinary individual. In addition, any distributions of corporate profits to the shareholders of the corporation are also subject to taxation as income to the individual. Thus, corporate income may be taxed twice.

A corporation can be created only by complying with the requirements of your individual State Corporation Code. Among the requirements of the Corporation Code are the following:

- Articles of Incorporation must be filed with the Secretary of State.

- Bylaws of the corporation must be adopted.

- The corporation must adhere to certain corporate formalities dictated by the Code, for example, the frequency and procedures surrounding shareholder meetings, the election of the board of directors, maintenance of certain cooperate records, etc.

Although many of the formalities dictated by the Corporation Code may seem unnecessary for the small corporation, compliance may be essential to maintaining the limited liability enjoyed by the corporation's shareholders.

A corporation may require the capital necessary to begin and continue operation of the business by two different means. Equity financing involves the insurance of shares of stock, which represent an ownership interest in the business, in exchange for cash, property, labor or services rendered. The primary advantage to the corporation of equity financing is that the corporation is not required to repay the principal or interest.

Instead, the shareholder acquires an interest in the business and may share in its future profits. In addition, since the investment received by the corporation constitutes equity, it may be used by the corporation for purposes of acquiring additional capital. On the other hand, the investor who becomes a shareholder in exchange for his/her investment has not guarantee of repayment. If the corporation is successful in the future, the shareholder may receive periodic distributions of the corporation's profits in the form of dividends.

Dividends are taxable of the shareholder as ordinary income. If the corporation repurchases its shares from the shareholder, the shareholder may also be taxed.

The corporation may also acquire capital by borrowing money. Debt financing is attractive to the investors because the corporation is legally obligated to repay the principal and interest. Interest payments are deductible to the corporation, thus avoiding the double taxation problem. These characteristics of debt financing which are attractive to investors are generally unappealing to the new corporation which has little cash and no present earnings.

F. S. Corporation

An S Corporation is one that does not pay a corporate tax on its income, but divides the expenses and income of the corporation among its shareholders. Shareholders report these expenses as income on their personal income tax returns.

Advantages of an S Corporation include the possibility of a lower tax rate because earnings are taxed at the individual shareholder's rate. Transfer of stock ownership can be made without transferring voting rights. In addition, when an S Corporation has a bad year, its shareholder can carry back three years and carry forward 15 years of their proportionate share of the loss in excess of their current year income.

To qualify as an S Corporation, a business must:

-   Be a domestic corporation. It cannot be a member of an affiliated group of corporations and must not have a subsidiary. It cannot be a domestic international sales corporation, a financial institution that takes deposits or makes loans, or a corporation which takes the tax credit for doing business in a U. S. possession.

-   Have only one class of stock issued and outstanding.

-   Not earn more than 25 percent of its gross receipts from passive investment sources during any three consecutive three-year periods. Passive investment income includes gross receipts from royalties, rents dividends, interest, annuities and sales or exchange of stock or securities.

-   Have a tax year ending December 31, unless the IRS can be convinced otherwise.

-   Have a maximum of 25 shareholders. Only individuals and their estates, and owners or beneficiaries of certain trusts may be shareholders. Shareholders must either be either U.S. citizens or president aliens; all shareholders must agree to elect S Corporation status.

Any domestic corporation may elect S Corporation status by filing with the IRS on Form 2553. Election by a Small Business Corporation. This election will only be valid if all shareholders have signed on this form their consent to the S Corporation status. The election must be filed on or before the 15th day of the third month of the current tax year.

Once elected, S Corporation status will continue until:

-   The corporation's shareholders revoke the choice, or the corporation no longer meets all of the requirements for S Corporations with earnings and profits violations.

–   The passive investment income restrictions on corporations will earnings and profits are violated.

For more details on qualifying and filing as an S corporation, contact your local IRS office and ask for IRS Publication #589, "Tax Information on S Corporation."

CONCLUSION

For the person considering starting a small business, choosing the most appropriate legal form for the business will require careful assessment of the characteristics of each form along with the needs and desires of those staring the business. Which the business be owned and operated by the single individual will not requiring the great deal of capital, the informality of the sole proprietorship may be most appropriate. If the business will be owned by two or more, a general partnership offers a means of polling the resources of each and sharing control of the business. There is relatively little formality required to establish and run the business, and control remains with the partners. Establishment of a limited partnership allows the business to acquire additional capital while avoiding the need to borrow and without surrendering control of the business.

Adoption of the corporate form, with its required formalities, may be a bit unwieldy for small businesses just getting started. The limited liability enjoyed by shareholders may appear attractive, but for the small business, most creditors will probably require that personal assets be put up as collateral anyway.

On the other hand, the ability to acquire capital by issuing stock may be very practical means of financing the business.

Selection of a business format requires a careful evaluation of both the present and probable future needs of the enterprise. To avoid duplication of legal expenses and the creation of entities which will not serve the long-term needs of the enterprise, the business founder should carefully analyze available options at the outset of the business, rather than stumble into an unsuitable or unwieldy business format solely by virtue of short-term convenience.

_____

_____

_____

_____

_____

_____

_____

_____

_____

14.   COMMUNITY BENEFITS

The proposed venture should be an instrument of community and human development as well as economic development, and it should be responsive to the expressed desires of the community.

Describe and discuss the potential economic and non-economic benefits to members of the community that could result from the formation of the proposed venture.

_____

_____

_____

Among the benefits that may merit discussion are:

Economic

Number of jobs generated in each of the first three years of the venture

_____

_____

_____

Number and kind of new employment opportunities for previously unemployed or underemployed individuals.

_____

_____

_____

Number of skilled and higher paying jobs

_____

_____

_____

Ownership and control of venture assets by community residents

_____

_____

_____

Purchase of goods and services from local suppliers

_____

_____

_____

Human Development

New technical skills development and associated career opportunities for community residents _____

_____

_____

Management development and training_____

_____

_____

Employment of unique skills within the community that are now unused._____

_____

_____

Community Development

Development of Community's physical assets_____

_____

_____

Improved perception of CDC responsiveness and its role in the community

_____

_____

_____

Provision of needed, but unsupplied, services or products to community

_____

_____

_____

Improvements in the living environment _____

_____

_____

Community support, participation and pride in venture _____

_____

_____

Development of community-owned economic structure and decreased absentee business ownership _____

_____

_____

Describe any compromises or time lags in venture profitability that may result from trying to achieve some or all of the kinds of benefits cited above. Any such compromises or lags in profitability should be justified in the context of all the benefits achieved and the role of the venture in a total, planned program of economic, human and community development.

_____

_____

_____

_____

_____

_____

_____

_____

II.   THE FINANCIAL PLAN

The purpose of the financial plan is to sufficiently inform the reader of the vial financial information on your business. If you have not had experience in preparing financial information it is important that you discuss this information with a qualified individual, or you may need to pay a professional to prepare this section of your business plan.

A. Loan Description

This includes the amount of many, the length of the loan, the desired terms, how you will use the money, how you are going to pay it back available collateral, and how will you pay it back if something goes wrong.

_____

_____

_____

B. Capital Equipment List

This includes equipment used to manufacture or deliver your product or service (not equipment or merchandise you sell directly to a customer). Include manufacturing machinery, delivery fleets, permanent fixtures such as special lighting, air conditioning, as well as office equipment like computers, desk, etc. If the proceeds of the requested loan go to purchase some of this equipment, list items purchased in detail. On a separate page, list equipment already owned.

_____

_____

_____

_____

_____

_____

_____

In development the financial plan, five basic exhibits must be prepared:

a. Profit and loss forecast for three years
b. Cash flow projection for three years
c. Pro forma balance sheet for three years
d. Sources of capital funds (initial and projected)
e. Historic financial data for existing business

Sample forms for preparing these have been provided as Appendixes. It is recommended that the venture's financial and marketing personnel prepare them with assistance from accountants and the venture packages required.

In addition to these five basic financial appendixes, a break-even chart should be presented that shows the level of first-year production that is required to cover <u>all</u> operating costs.

A. Profit and Loss Forecast

The preparation of a pro forma income statement is the planning-for-profit part of financial management. Crucial to the earnings forecast—as well as other projections—is the sales forecast. An income statement defines the relationship among revenues, expenses, and the resulting profit or loss. Revenues and expenses are generated through operating transactions and financial transactions: therefore, the complete income statement must be developed in two phases.

The first phase is to estimate the firm's operating income.

_____

_____

_____

_____

_____

_____

_____

The second phase focuses on the impact of financial transactions on the income.

_____

_____

_____

_____

_____

_____

_____

The process must move in two phases because the impact of financial transactions on income cannot be computed until a firm knows the effect of operations on its financial and capital structure positions.

Once the sales forecast is in hand, production or operations for a service business should be budgeted. There must be a determination of the level of production or operation that is required to meet the sales forecast and fulfill inventory requirements. The material, labor, service and equipment requirements must be developed and translated into cost data.

Separation of the fixed and variable elements of these costs is desirable and the effect for sales volume on inventory, equipment acquisitions and manufacturing costs must be taken into account. Sales expense should include the costs of selling and distribution, storage, discounts, advertising and promotions.

_____

_____

_____

_____

_____

General and administrative expense should include management salaries, secretarial costs, and legal and accounting expenses.

_____

_____

_____

Manufacturing or operations overhead includes rent, utilities, fringe benefits, telephone, etc. Earnings projections should be prepared monthly in the first year of operation and quarterly for the second and third year.

_____

_____

_____

In addition to serving as a basis for planning, the projected income statements can be used for operating control functions. Through comparisons with actual operating control functions, through comparisons with actual operating sales and profit information, the operating status of the venture can be determined relative to the objectives that have been se out in the plan. This type of analysis can be used by management to indicate critical factors which need attention and can indicate the need for a reassessment of the underlying assumptions used to develop the projections.

_____

_____

_____

_____

_____

_____

Discussion of Assumptions

Because of the importance of profit and loss projection as an indication to potential investors of the potential financial feasibility of any new venture, it is extremely important that the assumptions made in its preparation be fully explained and documented. If the statements are to be useful, they must represent management's realistic assessment and best estimates of probable operating results. Sales or operational cost projections that are either too conservative or too optimistic have little value as aids to policy formulation and decision-making. Thinking about assumptions before start-up is useful for identifying issues which require consideration before they turn into major problems.

_____

_____

_____

_____

_____

_____

As well ad explanations for the projected sales growth, include any assumptions made about costs of sales expense, such as materials purchases, direct labor manufacturing overhead, etc., and general and administrative expenses. These assumptions should be attached to the earning projections.

_____

_____

_____

_____

Risks and Sensitivity

Once the income statements have been prepared, discuss the major risks that could prevent those goals from being attained and the sensitivity of profits to these risks.

_____

_____

_____

_____

This discussion should reflect the business' thinking about some of the risks that might be encountered in the firm itself, the industry, and the environment. This should include things such as the different effects a twenty percent reduction in sales projections will have on the impact of learning requirements for management and non-management employees and how it will affect the level of productivity over time.

_____

_____

_____

_____

B. Pro Forma Cash Flow Analysis

The purpose of a cash-flow statement is to evaluate the impact of an operations and financing structure on the cash position of a business. In general, businesses must have sufficient cash to cover their financial obligations at any time. For a new business the cash flow forecast is more important than the forecast of profits because it details the amount and timing of expected cash in-flow and out-flows. Usually the level of profits, particularly during the start-up years of a business, will not be sufficient to finance operating needs. Moreover, cash in-flow does not match the outflow on a short-term basis. The cash flow forecast will indicate these conditions and enable management to plan cash needs.

Given a level of projected sales and capital expenditures over a specific period, the cash flow forecast will highlight the need for additional financing and indicate peak requirements for working capital. Management must decide how this additional financing is to be obtained, on what terms, and how it is to be repaid. This information becomes part of the final cash flow forecast.

If the business is in a seasonal or cyclical industry or an industry in which suppliers require a new firm to pay cash or if inventory build-up occurs before the product can be sold for revenues-this cash forecast is crucial to the continuing solvency of the business. A detailed cash flow forecast which is understood and used by management can enable them to direct their attention to operating problems without distractions caused by periodic crises which should have been anticipated.

Cash flow projections should be made for each month of the first fiscal year of operation and quarterly for the second and third years.

_____

_____

_____

_____

_____

_____

_____

Discussion of Assumptions

This should include assumptions made about the collection of receivable timetables, trade discounts given, terms of payments to vendors, planned salary and wage increases, anticipated increases in other operating expenses, seasonal characteristics of the business as they affect inventory requirements, and capital equipment purchases. As with sales and income projections, it is important that these assumptions represent management's best estimates. These assumptions should be attached to the projected cash flow forecasts.

_____

_____

_____

_____

_____

_____

_____

_____

_____

_____

_____

_____

_____

_____

Cash Flow Sensitivity

Once the cash flow forecast has been completed, discuss the implications for funds needs caused by possible changes in some of the crucial assumptions. This is designed to enable the business to test the sensitivity of the cash budget to a variety of assumptions about business factors and to view a wider range of possible outcomes.

_____

_____

_____

_____

_____

_____

C. Pro Forma Balance Sheet

This provides a snapshot view of what you own, and what you own, and what you owe at a particular point in time. Contains the same categories of information, regardless of the type of business. Assets should be ranked in a decreasing order of liquidity, while liabilities should be listed in a decreasing order from the most immediate. The following is a sample outline of a balance sheet.

Assets
  – Current Assets
  – Fixed Assets
  – Other Assets
  – Total Assets

Liabilities
  – Current Liabilities
  – Long-term Liabilities
  – Total Liabilities
  – Net Worth (total Assets minus total liabilities)
    Total Liabilities and Net Worth

Discussion of Assumptions

Discuss any new assumptions underlying the preparation of these statements.

D. Break-Even Chart

Break-Even analysis allows you to demonstrate when your business will reach its break-even point—when sales will reach the level which covers all expenses. A basic break-even formula is:

$$S = FC + VC$$

S (break eve level of sales in dollars) = FC (Fixed costs, those which remain constant such as rent and salaries) + VC (variable costs, such as the cost of the sale, including commission, delivery of the product and the costs of the product sold).

A break-even analysis can tell you quickly if your costs are too high, or if the price of your product or services is too low.

_____

_____

_____

_____

_____

_____

_____

_____

_____

_____

_____

_____

15.   PROPOSED FINANCING

This section is to be devoted to a discussion of the current and proposed capital structure of the business and to a summary of management's conclusions about the timing and probable sources of funds to meet peak cash requirements. Preparation of this section should be structured so that the following issues are covered:

Identification of the initial equity investors by name, amount invested, and shares received, and at what cost. _____

_____

_____

_____

_____

Initial long-term debt, interest rate, repayments terms, and source.

_____

_____

_____

Description of the type of funding requested.

_____

_____

_____

Description of how the capital funds will be allocated to the various business operations. Approximately how will the finds be used—working capital, equipment purchases, debt repayment (if any), to cover projected operating losses, etc.

_____

_____

_____

Based on the cash flow forecast, include management's conclusions about the timing of peak cash needs and how these requirements will be met. For example, secure a line of credit with a local bank, take on additional long-term debt, attracting new equity investors, consider factors receivable, or any combination of these.

_____

_____

_____

_____

Describe any plans for distributing all or a portion of the stock of the company to the residents of the community. Give the estimated timing and amounts of such distribution.

_____

_____

_____

_____

_____

_____

_____

_____

_____

_____

_____

III.   SUPPORTING DOCUMENTS

The purpose of this section is to provide detailed information supporting the claims that you have made in the body of the business plan. This area should include the following information:

- Personal resumes
- Employee contracts
- Job descriptions
- Personal financial statements
- Patents, Trademarks, or Copyrights
- Agreements
- Brochures
- Logos
- Market Research
- Photographs
- Operational Plans
- Customer Plans
- Demographic Information
- Product Description
- Credit reports
- Letters of reference
- Copies of leases
- Contracts (legal documents)
- And anything else of relevance to the plan

PUT YOU PLAN INTO ACTION

When your plan is as on target as possible, you are ready to put it into action. Keep in mind that action is not acted upon, it is of no more value than a pleasant dream that evaporated over breakfast coffee.

A successful entrepreneur does not stop after he/she has gathered information and drawn up a plan, as you have done in working through this outline. He/she begins to use this plan.

At this point, look back over your plan. Look for things that must be done to put your plan into action.

In the spaces that follow, list things that must be done to put your plan into action. Give each item a date so that it can be done at the appropriate time. To put my plan into action I must do the following:

Action   Completion Date

_____   _____

_____   _____

_____   _____

_____   _____

_____   _____

_____   _____

_____   _____

_____   _____

_____   _____

KEEP YOUR PLAN UP TO DATE

Once you put your plan into action, look out for changes.
They can cripple the best-made business plan if the entrepreneur lets them.

Stay on top of changing conditions and adjust your business plan accordingly.

In order to adjust your plan to account for change, an entrepreneur must:

(1) Be alert to the changes that come in your company, line of business, market and customers.

(2) Check your plan against these changes.

(3) Determine what revisions; if any are needed in you plan.

The method you use to keep your plan current so that your business can weather the forces of the market place is up to you. Read the trade papers and magazines for your line of business. Another suggestions concerns your time. Set aside some time—two hours, three hours, whatever is necessary to review your plan? Once each month, or every other month, go over the plan to see whether it needs adjusting. If revisions are needed, make them and put them into action.

GOOD LUCK ON YOUR NEW VENTURE:

Gary M. Thomas, MBA, BSBA – Adjunct Instructor. Gary graduated from Columbia College with a Bachelor Degree in Business Administration and earned his Master's Degree from the University of Phoenix. Gary has been involved in all aspects of the mortuary and funeral business including funeral home ownership and management. His experience includes both family and corporate owned funeral homes and cemeteries.

Currently, Gary is an Assistant Manager for Fairmount Mortuary. He is on the Vice President of the Colorado Funeral Directors Association.

He has over 15 years of experience with a Fortune 500 company in management and marketing. Gary has been teaching at numerous colleges in the Denver area the past twelve years, winning multiple awards as the 'Outstanding Instructor'. Gary has also published magazine articles on the funeral service business.

Why should you go to the trouble of creating a written business plan? There are three major reasons:

1. The process of putting a business plan together, including the thought you put in before Beginning to write it, forces you to take an objective, critical unemotional look at your business project in its entirety.

2. The finished product your business plan is and operating told which, properly used, will help you manage your business and work toward its success.

3. The completed business plan is the means for communicating your ideas to others and provide the basis for your financing proposal.

The importance of planning cannot be overemphasized. By taking an objective look at your business you can identify areas of weakness and strengths, pinpoint needs you might otherwise overlook, spot problems before they arise, and begin planning how you can best achieve your business goals. As an operating tool, your business plan helps you to establish reasonable objectives and figure out how to best accomplish them. It also helps you to red-flag problems as they arise and aids you to identifying their sources, thus suggesting ways to solve them. It may even help you avoid some problems altogether.

This handbook has been designed with these considerations in mind. In order for it to work it is important that you do as much of the work as possible. A professionally prepared business plan won't do you any good if you don't understand it thoroughly. This understanding comes from being involved with its development from the very start.

No business plan, no matter how carefully constructed and no matter how thoroughly understood, will be of any use at all unless you use it. Going into business is rough; over half of all new businesses fail within the first two years of operation and over 90 percent fail within the first 10 years. A major reason for failure is lack of planning. The best way to enhance your chances of success is to plan and follow through on your planning.

Use your plan. Don't put it in the bottom drawer of your desk and forget it.

Your business plan can help you avoid going into a business venture that is doomed to failure. If your proposed venture is marginal at best, the business plan will show you why and may help you avoid paying the high tuition of business failure. It is far cheaper not to begin an ill-fated business than to learn by experience what your business plan could have taught you at several hours of concentrated work.

Finally, your business plan provides the information needed by others to evaluate your venture, especially if you need to seek outside financing. A thorough business automatically becomes a complete financing proposal which will meet the requirements of most lenders.